URSA

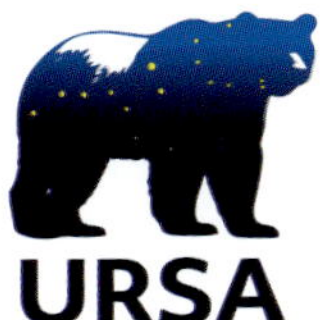

Where You DARE Not Go

Alarming Afterlife

SCARY CEMETERIES AND GRAVEYARDS

by

Judy Allen and Dinah Williams

BEARPORT PUBLISHING

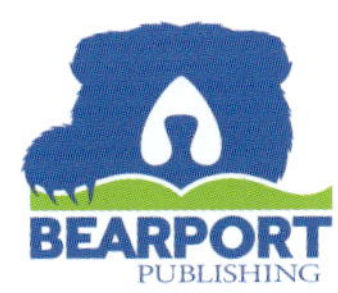

Minneapolis, Minnesota

Credits
Cover and title page, © Creaturart Images/Shutterstock and © d1sk/Shutterstock; 4, © Fer Gregory/Shutterstock, © Anna Kucherova/Shutterstock, and © fon.tepsoda/Shutterstock; 6, © Netfalls/Adobe Stock; 7, © Wyatt Rivard/Shutterstock; 8, © Juan Pablo Hinojosa/Adobe Stock and © Maggie Royle/iStock; 9, © NikhomTreeVector/Shutterstock; 10, © Michael Howser/Wirestock Creators/Adobe Stock and © tacojim/iStock; 11, © Brunk Auctions/Wikimedia Commons and © Fer Gregory/Shutterstock; 12, © Luis Boudat Ducollier /Wikimedia Commons; 13, © powerofforever/iStock and © Ondřej Mangl/Wikimedia Commons; 14, © SochAnam/iStock and © Everett Collection/Shutterstock; 15, © Christine_Kohler/iStock; 16, © Kamira/Shutterstock and © clivewa/Shutterstock; 17, © Kamira/Shutterstock; 18, © Business Wire / Handout/Getty Images, © Apic / Contributor/Getty Images, and © Universal History Archive / Contributor/Getty Images; 19, © LukeandKarla.Travel/Shutterstock; 20, © Swampyank/Creative Commons Attribution-Share Alike 3.0 Unported; 21, © Kiselev Andrey Valerevich/Shutterstock; 22, © Mick Sinclair/Alamy; 23, © Metropolitan Police Archives/Wikimedia Commons; 24, © MrHarman/Creative Commons Attribution-Share Alike 3.0 Unported; 25, © Lakersnbulls91/Creative Commons Attribution-Share Alike 3.0 Unported; 26, © photographereddie/iStock; 27, © Ungor/Shutterstock and © Rosamar/Shutterstock; 28, © ikeby/Adobe Stock; 29, © Carolyn M Carpenter/Shutterstock and © Creativa Images/Shutterstock; 30, © Mark Bergner/Creative Commons Attribution-Share Alike 4.0 International; 31, © smereka/Shutterstock and © Patrick Jennings/Shutterstock; 32, © Rocketrod1960/Wikimedia Commons; 33, © Master1305/Shutterstock; 34, © Guillermo Olaizola/Shutterstock; 35, © LanKS/Shutterstock, © True Touch Lifestyle/Shutterstock, and © Everett Collection/Shutterstock; 36, © 2112guy/Wikimedia Commons; 37, © Anneka/Shutterstock and © 2112guy/Wikimedia Commons; 38, © Alex Segre/Adobe Stock; 39, © Rubanitor/Shutterstock; 40, © Vintagepix/Shutterstock; 41, © Dennis Jarvis/Creative Commons Attribution-Share Alike 2.0 Generic and © Kateryna Mashkevych/Shutterstock; 42–43, © maodoltee/Shutterstock.

Bearport Publishing Company Product Development Team
President: Jen Jenson; Director of Product Development: Spencer Brinker; Managing Editor: Allison Juda; Associate Editor: Naomi Reich; Associate Editor: Tiana Tran; Art Director: Colin O'Dea; Designer: Kim Jones; Designer: Kayla Eggert; Product Development Assistant: Owen Hamlin

Statement on Usage of Generative Artificial Intelligence
Bearport Publishing remains committed to publishing high-quality nonfiction books. Therefore, we restrict the use of generative AI to ensure accuracy of all text and visual components pertaining to a book's subject. See BearportPublishing.com for details.

Library of Congress Cataloging-in-Publication Data

Names: Allen, Judy, author. | Williams, Dinah (Dinah J.) author.
Title: Alarming afterlife : scary cemeteries and graveyards / by Judy Allen and Dinah Williams.
Description: Minneapolis, Minnesota : Bearport Publishing Company, [2025] | Series: Where you dare not go | Includes bibliographical references and index.
Identifiers: LCCN 2023059732 (print) | LCCN 2023059733 (ebook) | ISBN 9798892320719 (library binding) | ISBN 9798892326032 (paperback) | ISBN 9798892322041 (ebook)
Subjects: LCSH: Haunted cemeteries--Juvenile literature. | Urban folklore--Juvenile literature.
Classification: LCC BF1474.3 .A445 2025 (print) | LCC BF1474.3 (ebook) | DDC 133.1/22--dc23/eng/20240126
LC record available at https://lccn.loc.gov/2023059732
LC ebook record available at https://lccn.loc.gov/2023059733

For more information, write to Bearport Publishing, 5357 Penn Avenue South, Minneapolis, MN 55419.

Contents

A Place to Rest?

By day, graveyards often look like peaceful parks filled with rolling lawns and tall trees. At night, things change. Moonlight casts an eerie glow on the headstones. Trees form creepy shapes and shadows. Suddenly, there's a noise! Out of the corner of your eye, you notice a dark figure creeping toward you, closer and closer. You realize that a cemetery isn't, perhaps, a place to rest in peace. . . .

The Empire of the Dead

CATACOMBS OF PARIS
PARIS, FRANCE

What is the spookiest thing about graveyards? For many people, it is the thought of thousands of bodies buried below their feet. Yet what happens when a city runs out of space to bury its dead? In the late 1700s, the people of Paris found out. . . .

Skulls and bones in the Paris catacombs

The graveyards of Paris had become too crowded. There was no longer room to bury the dead below ground, so people started stacking the corpses on top of one another aboveground. They piled them almost 10 feet (3 m) high inside cemetery walls. The weight of the bodies broke through in some places, however. Corpses spilled into the street. The smell of their rotting flesh made people sick.

The government needed a way to solve this problem. So, workers moved the corpses to a larger space. It was a huge job. From around 1785 to 1859, about six million bodies from cemeteries all over the city were dug up. They were reburied in ancient underground quarries that stretched for more than 180 miles (290 km) below the city. Stacks of skulls and bones still line the walls of these haunted catacombs.

A passageway in the catacombs

Today, thousands of visitors come every year to walk among the long-dead. Many tell of meeting ghostly figures roaming the dark passageways. A few unlucky visitors have gotten hopelessly lost among the bones. These people have never been found. Their bodies now rest forever in the Empire of the Dead.

The Vampire's Tree

EL PANTEÓN DE BELÉN
GUADALAJARA, MEXICO

In a small cemetery in Guadalajara, Mexico, there's a towering, twisted tree. If you look closely, you'll see that the huge tree appears to be growing out of a grave. Whose grave is it, and how did the mysterious tree get there?

The vampire's tree

El Panteón de Belén cemetery

More than 150 years ago, the people of Guadalajara, Mexico, began finding small dead animals scattered around the city. There was something very strange about the tiny corpses—they had been drained of their blood. Soon after, babies were found dead in their cribs. They, too, had been emptied of blood. People began to suspect that a vampire was feasting on their loved ones.

The people of Guadalajara feared for their lives. So, a group of brave townspeople decided to track down the vampire and put an end to the killings. One night, after a new corpse had been discovered, the group saw a strange man with pale skin creeping in the shadows. They were certain they had found their vampire. The townspeople grabbed the man and plunged a wooden stake through his heart. The next day, the people buried his body in a grave in El Panteón de Belén cemetery, with the stake still in place. They placed the body under heavy concrete to prevent it from rising from the dead.

Months later, the stake began to grow into a tree. Over the years, the tree split the concrete and grew to tower over the grave. Some people believe that if you break a branch off the tree, the vampire's blood will ooze out of it.

Today, a tall fence surrounds the tree to protect it. People say that if the tree is cut down or dies, the vampire will rise from the grave and kill again.

The Voodoo Queen of New Orleans

SAINT LOUIS CEMETERY NO. 1
NEW ORLEANS, LOUISIANA

New Orleans has more than 40 cemeteries scattered among its homes and businesses. These cities of the dead are so crowded that visitors who tour them are warned about getting lost. With the dead possibly outnumbering the living, it's no wonder that New Orleans is considered one of the most haunted places in America.

Saint Louis Cemetery No. 1

Marie Laveau's tomb

In the 1800s, Marie Laveau was New Orleans's greatest voodoo queen. She produced powerful charms and magical potions. She held services where people were taken over by spirits. She was even said to have saved a man sentenced to death by hanging. According to legend, Marie created a rainstorm that caused the hangman's noose to slip from the doomed man's neck.

Marie Laveau

Though dead for more than 125 years, people still go to Marie for help. They say that if you leave gifts and mark Xs on her tomb, she will cast spells to grant your wish.

Is the voodoo queen of New Orleans still giving help from beyond the grave? Head to Saint Louis Cemetery No. 1 to find out.

A voodoo doll

Most cemeteries in New Orleans have tombs where the dead are buried aboveground. Why? About half of the city is below sea level. If coffins were buried in the soggy ground, they could float up out of their graves.

Ghost Town Graves

LA NORIA CEMETERY, LA NORIA, CHILE

La Noria is a small abandoned town in Chile located in the driest place on Earth—the Atacama Desert. In the late 1800s, the people who lived in the town worked in mines harvesting a kind of salt called saltpeter. When the mines closed, the people moved away. Today, little is left of the town except broken machinery, derelict houses, graves, and . . . the occasional ghost.

An abandoned mine in La Noria

Life for La Noria's miners was very difficult. Their work was backbreaking, and the owners of the mine treated their workers very badly. As a result, many of the miners died young. They were then buried in shallow graves in the sandy soil of La Noria Cemetery. Over time, the hot desert wind has blown the sand from some of the graves, revealing whole skeletons with grinning skulls. Shreds of clothing still hang off the dry, jagged bones.

Some people claim that the spirits of the dead miners remain in the town. It is said that ghostly figures wander through the empty streets at night, and disembodied voices whisper and weep in the cemetery at dusk. Residents of the nearby town of Iquique warn visitors not to go to La Noria. They believe that the ghostly miners are looking for eternal companions.

Saltpeter

Saltpeter was once so valuable it was called white gold. In the past, it was made into gunpowder and fertilizer. Eventually, scientists discovered how to manufacture it. As a result, most of the saltpeter mines in Chile closed.

The Ghosts of Gettysburg

GETTYSBURG NATIONAL MILITARY PARK
GETTYSBURG, PENNSYLVANIA

A ghost is the spirit of a person who stays on Earth after death. Many ghosts are thought to haunt the place where they died violently or unexpectedly. For that reason, battlefields after a war are often haunted. Yet how does one explain a ghost visiting during a battle?

Gettysburg National Military Park

The Battle of Gettysburg

The Battle of Gettysburg was one of the deadliest battles of the U.S. Civil War (1861–1865). After only three bloody days of fighting in July 1863, about 50,000 soldiers were dead, wounded, or missing. Many were buried right where they fell. No wonder so many ghosts have been seen at this cemetery built on the site of a battlefield.

One of the most famous ghost sightings at Gettysburg, however, was of someone who had died many years before the famous battle. Soldiers from Maine were on their way to help other Northern soldiers fight the South. They became lost. The ghost of George Washington on a white horse suddenly appeared. He pointed them in the right direction. Some say word of his appearance boosted morale so much that it helped the North win the battle.

George Washington is not the only president whose ghost returned to haunt this world. The spirit of Abraham Lincoln has been seen a number of times in the White House.

George Washington on a horse

Beware of the Poltergeist!

GREYFRIARS KIRKYARD
EDINBURGH, SCOTLAND

Greyfriars Kirkyard is an old church graveyard that dates back to the 1500s. It was built on the site of an ancient monastery that was later used as a prison. Many of the gravestones in Greyfriars Kirkyard have skulls and other images of death carved into them, but something far more disturbing lingers in the old cemetery.

Greyfriars Kirkyard

The tomb of George Mackenzie

In the 1600s, King Charles II of England tried to force the Scottish people to change their religion. Many Scots refused. Disobeying the king, however, was against the law and resulted in arrest. A harsh judge named George Mackenzie forced the Scots who were arrested to await trial in a prison built in the churchyard. Many of the prisoners died from cold or starvation and were buried where they fell. Others were sentenced to death by the cruel judge. When Mackenzie finally died, he was buried in a tomb in Greyfriars Kirkyard. It's hardly surprising that a vicious poltergeist now haunts the place.

One night in 1998, a man broke into Mackenzie's tomb and damaged the judge's coffin. According to legend, the man awoke a spirit that should have been left alone. The poltergeist has pinched, bruised, and terrified many visitors. It can strike anywhere in the cemetery, but it is especially active near Mackenzie's tomb and inside the old prison. Guides who give tours of the graveyard always warn people to enter Greyfriars Kirkyard at their own risk.

A statue of Greyfriars Bobby

In the 1800s, a loyal dog named Greyfriars Bobby spent 14 years guarding his dead owner's grave at Greyfriars Kirkyard. Local people fed the terrier until he died and was buried near his deceased owner.

A Mummy's Curse

TUTANKHAMUN'S TOMB
VALLEY OF THE KINGS, EGYPT

It is said that people who disturb a mummy's tomb risk death. For more than 100 years, stories have been told of the mummy's curse. Are the legends true? For one person, it is too late to find out.

King Tut's coffin

Lord Carnarvon (*left*) with Howard Carter

Howard Carter (*left*) studying King Tut's coffin

In 1922, after five years of searching, Lord Carnarvon and Howard Carter had found it! They had uncovered the tomb of King Tutankhamun.

King Tut was a pharaoh who ruled Egypt for only nine years. He died at the age of 18 around 1322 BCE. At that time, Egyptians believed that a pharaoh's life continued among the gods after death. So, the boy-king was buried with everything he might need in the afterlife. King Tut's body was surrounded by treasures, including gold-covered chariots, bows and arrows, swords, and his golden throne. The pharaoh's tomb remained hidden in the Valley of the Kings for more than 3,000 years.

Lord Carnarvon's discovery of the pharaoh's dazzling treasure made him world-famous. He couldn't believe his luck. Yet less than six months later, Lord Carnarvon was dead. A simple mosquito bite led to pneumonia, which killed him. Some were puzzled by his strange death. Was he actually killed by a mummy's curse?

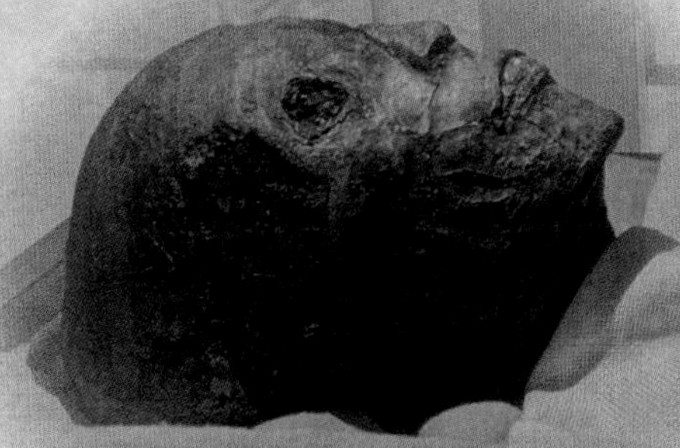

The Mummy of King Tut

The ancient Egyptians thought a person's spirit needed a home in the afterlife. So, they preserved the dead body as a mummy. Its insides, including the lungs and the stomach, were taken out and put in jars. The body was dried out using salt. It was then wrapped in cloth and placed in a coffin.

The Last American Vampire

CHESTNUT HILL CEMETERY
EXETER, RHODE ISLAND

Some people believe cemeteries are home to both the dead and the undead. Vampires are corpses that have come back to life. These undead creatures rise from their graves at night to drink the blood of the living. This keeps vampires alive forever, but it slowly kills their victims. One man decided to stop a vampire before she killed again.

Chestnut Hill Cemetery Church

George Brown felt cursed. In the early 1880s, he watched helplessly as consumption killed both his wife and his daughter Mary. Around 1891, his son, Edwin, also got the disease. The next year, one of George's other daughters, Mercy, also fell ill and died.

After Mercy's funeral, Edwin became weaker. George was terrified of losing his only son. He began to consider whether there was any truth to the vampire legend. Could Mercy have become a vampire? Was she sucking the life out of her brother, Edwin?

Desperate, George opened Mercy's coffin at Chestnut Hill Cemetery. Though she'd been dead for months, Mercy looked surprisingly the same as when she was alive. Perhaps she really was a vampire.

To end Mercy's power over Edwin, George cut out her heart and burned it. He then fed the ashes to his son. Unfortunately, this did not save Edwin. He died within two months, on May 2, 1892. To this day, Mercy is still considered by many to be the most famous—and perhaps the last—American vampire.

A vampire

During the 1800s, one out of four people died from consumption. Like the victim of a vampire attack, a person with consumption becomes pale, stops eating, and wastes away.

The Gliding Nun

BARNES OLD CEMETERY, LONDON, ENGLAND

Barnes Old Cemetery is half hidden among trees and tangled ivy in a London park. In the late 1870s, the victim of a violent murder was buried in the cemetery. Ever since that time, there have been reports of a pale nun-like figure gliding back and forth among the headstones. Who is she, and what is she looking for?

A headless statue at Barnes Old Cemetery

In 1879, something horrifying washed up on the shores of the River Thames, near Barnes Old Cemetery. It was a box containing the bones of a woman. However, one important piece of the skeleton was missing—the skull. Because the woman was never identified, her bones were buried in an unmarked grave. That's when the gliding white figure of a nun was first seen at Barnes Old Cemetery.

Later, it was discovered that the skeleton was that of 55-year-old Julia Martha Thomas, who had lived near the River Thames in the late 1800s. In 1879, Mrs. Thomas hired a maid named Kate Webster, who had a criminal past and a bad temper. Kate admitted that after an argument with Mrs. Thomas, Kate became so angry that she pushed Mrs. Thomas down the stairs and killed her. Kate got rid of the body by cutting it up, removing the head, and then boiling the flesh off the bones. Finally, she put the bones inside a box and tossed it into the river.

Is the ghostly figure at the Barnes Old Cemetery not a nun after all? Could it be the spirit of Mrs. Thomas, hovering over her grave?

In 2010, Mrs. Thomas's skull was discovered buried in a garden near her old house.

Kate Webster, the murderer

Resurrection Mary

RESURRECTION CEMETERY, JUSTICE, ILLINOIS

Ghosts are thought to be spirits that cannot rest in peace. Some mingle with the living for a short time before returning to their graves. People who live near Chicago have been telling stories about one such ghost for more than 75 years.

Resurrection Cemetery

If a woman in a white dress is hitchhiking on Archer Avenue, don't stop the car! Most likely, it's the ghost many call Resurrection Mary. She was killed in a car crash around 1930 while hitchhiking home from a night of dancing. Mary has been seen dozens of times since being buried in Resurrection Cemetery.

One of the most famous sightings happened in 1939. Jerry Palus met Mary at a dance hall. They spent the evening dancing together. Jerry noticed, however, that Mary was strangely cold to the touch. When he drove her home, Mary asked him to stop at Resurrection Cemetery. She said, "Where I'm going, you can't follow." She threw open the car door and ran toward the cemetery. Before reaching the gates, however, she disappeared before Jerry's eyes.

In the 1970s and 1980s, the number of people who claimed to see Mary increased. During this time, Resurrection Cemetery was being renovated. Perhaps the people working there disturbed Mary, making her more restless than ever.

The bent bars of the gate at Resurrection Cemetery

In 1976, a woman wearing a white dress was seen clutching the bars of the gates outside Resurrection Cemetery. Police later found the bars bent. Two small handprints were burned into the metal. Was it Mary trying to get out?

The Haunted Road and the Hanged Man

EL CAMPO SANTO CEMETERY
SAN DIEGO, CALIFORNIA

El Campo Santo, which means the holy field in Spanish, is a cemetery in San Diego that was built in the mid-1800s on land that once belonged to Native Americans. The first people buried in the cemetery were pioneer families. In 1889, a street was built through it, covering at least 20 graves. Many people believe this awoke and angered the spirits of the dead.

Graves at El Campo Santo Cemetery

People who live near El Campo Santo Cemetery have noticed some very strange things. Car alarms blare for no obvious reason, and cars that are parked near the cemetery often break down. Some people claim they feel an icy chill in the air, even on the hottest days.

What's even stranger is the tall, shadowy figure who lingers around one of the graves. The ghost is thought to be Yankee Jim Robinson. In 1852, Yankee Jim was convicted of stealing a boat. He was sentenced to death and hanged from a gallows. "He swung back and forth like a pendulum until he strangled to death," according to a local newspaper reporter. Yankee Jim's body was then buried in the cemetery. Just before his execution, Yankee Jim cried out that he was innocent. Is this why his spirit is not at peace?

The street that now covers some of the graves at El Campo Santo Cemetery is called San Diego Avenue.

Visitors to the cemetery sometimes see a Native American dressed in traditional clothes. Many people think he is the cemetery watchman. When they ask him a question, however, he simply disappears.

The Hollywood Vampire

HOLLYWOOD CEMETERY
RICHMOND, VIRGINIA

Sometimes a person's final resting place is neither a graveyard nor a cemetery. A tragic accident can suddenly turn a train tunnel into a tomb. Could the fear of being trapped underground have turned one man into a monster?

Hollywood Cemetery

In 1925, the Church Hill train tunnel collapsed below the city of Richmond, Virginia. A crew had been working on the tunnel to make it wider so that larger trains could pass through it. More than 200 people were at work when the tunnel collapsed. Many were able to find safety belowground. There are reports, however, of someone who found a way to escape.

Legend says a strange creature clawed his way out of the caved-in tunnel. His mouth was covered with blood. His teeth were jagged, and strips of skin hung from his arms and legs.

The creature ran to nearby Hollywood Cemetery and crawled into a crypt. Was it a vampire? Had it been feasting on the bodies of those trapped underground? Or was it just one of the workers who stumbled out of the tunnel with burned skin falling off his body? No one knows for sure.

One statue in Hollywood Cemetery is said to have a life of its own. In the 1800s, a father placed an iron statue of a dog next to his daughter's grave. According to legend, the dog guards the young girl, coming to life and chasing people away from her resting place.

The House That Haunts

BACHELOR'S GROVE CEMETERY
CHICAGO, ILLINOIS

Near a thick forest in a suburb of Chicago is Bachelor's Grove Cemetery. It's not just any cemetery. In fact, it's one of the most haunted places in the United States. There have been more than 100 documented reports of ghostly sightings there, including a phantom farmhouse that disappears and then reappears.

Bachelor's Grove Cemetery

You've probably heard of haunted houses, but have you heard of a house that haunts? According to witnesses, there's a white two-story farmhouse nestled among some trees near the cemetery. A lamp burns brightly in the upstairs window. When visitors walk toward the building, however, it shrinks before their very eyes! Then, it disappears into thin air. According to legend, if you try to enter the house, you will be trapped inside . . . forever.

In addition to the disappearing house, drivers on a road near the cemetery have spotted orbs of blue light dancing among the trees. They have also seen a fast-moving red light that looks like a streak of blood in the sky. In the 1970s, forest rangers on night watch noticed something even more peculiar at a nearby pond. They saw the ghostly image of an old man driving a horse and plow out of the pond. The rangers had no idea that in the 1870s, an old man lived nearby and used a horse to plow his fields. One day, something scared his horse, and it galloped straight into the pond. The man was caught in the reins. He couldn't free himself or the horse from the heavy plow, and they both drowned.

In 1991, a group of ghost hunters explored the cemetery after dark. They saw nothing unusual but took infrared photographs. One photo revealed a partly see-through woman sitting on a gravestone.

Voices from the Mausoleum

TOOWONG CEMETERY, BRISBANE, AUSTRALIA

Sometimes a person with a troubled past is unable to rest after he or she dies. That person may decide to haunt and torment the living. Could this be what happened to a butcher named Patrick Mayne who lived in Australia in the 1800s?

The mausoleum of the Mayne family in Toowong Cemetery

In 1848, police found the bloody remains of Robert Cox, a woodcutter. Robert had been murdered and then butchered into small pieces. Part of his body was dumped in the Brisbane River. His severed head was found in a nearby shed. According to police, Robert had just been paid for months of work, yet the large amount of money he was carrying was missing.

Patrick Mayne, a butcher with a violent temper, was suspected of the crime. He and Robert had recently been spotted together at a pub, and Patrick needed money to open a new butcher shop. It's believed that Patrick framed another man for the murder. That man was later found guilty and hanged.

When Patrick died, he was buried in a large, white mausoleum in Toowong Cemetery. Whether or not Patrick was guilty, the mausoleum is a frightening place. The air around it is often unexpectedly chilly. Visitors have claimed to hear thumps, angry voices, and crashes from deep inside the mausoleum. Could the sounds be coming from Patrick's restless spirit?

Patrick Mayne is believed to have been mentally ill. His five children never married or had children. Perhaps they feared passing down their father's sickness.

Poe's Phantom Visitor

WESTMINSTER BURYING GROUNDS
BALTIMORE, MARYLAND

Cemeteries are more than just a collection of graves. They are reminders of each person's time on Earth. Some people travel far and wide to pay tribute to their dead heroes. One mysterious stranger not only visits a grave, but also comes bringing gifts.

This tombstone marks the place where Poe was buried in 1849.

For more than 150 years, Edgar Allan Poe's tales of horror have terrified readers. Many of his stories deal with death and violence. In 1849, the writer was found lying unconscious in a street in Baltimore, Maryland. He was rushed to a hospital. Less than a week later, he died and was buried. No one knows exactly what caused his death.

Since 1949, a dark figure has haunted Poe's grave. Every year on the author's birthday, the stranger appears. The mysterious man is dressed in black and arrives just after midnight. He silently raises a glass in a birthday toast to Poe. When he leaves, he places three red roses at Poe's grave. Although he has been photographed, a hat and scarf always hide his face. To this day, no one is sure who he is.

Edgar Allan Poe

One of Edgar Allan Poe's most terrifying tales is "The Tell-Tale Heart." The narrator of the story kills an old man and buries him under the floorboards. When the police come, the murderer imagines that he can still hear the dead man's beating heart. Desperate to make the sound stop, he confesses to the crime.

The Woman in White

UNION CEMETERY, EASTON, CONNECTICUT

The Union Cemetery in Easton dates back to the 1700s and lies where three major roads meet. It is said to be the most haunted location in Connecticut. Phantom voices and mysterious glowing orbs have been reported in or near the cemetery. Unexplained streaks and blurs of light have appeared on photographs taken by visitors. The ghostly sightings are not only reported from within the cemetery but also spill out onto the roadways. People often report seeing a phantom woman in white leaping in front of their cars.

Union Cemetery

Visitors say that Union Cemetery is haunted by a mysterious woman with long dark hair wearing a white nightgown. She is the Woman in White and has been spotted floating among the gravestones. No one knows who she was when she was alive. Some think she was murdered and her body was dumped in the cemetery. Others believe she is the spirit of a woman who murdered her husband and then killed herself. A third story says she died giving birth and is looking for her baby.

Whoever she is, the spirit has frightened many cemetery visitors, as well as people driving nearby. Sometimes, she appears suddenly, right in front of a moving car. Horrified drivers slam on their brakes and leap out of their cars to check for a body. Yet the woman has vanished, and all they find is an empty road.

People are not allowed inside Union Cemetery after sundown. However, at night, ghost hunters sometimes take photographs through the fence that surrounds the graves. Some photos have shown what is thought to be spirit energy rising from the tombs.

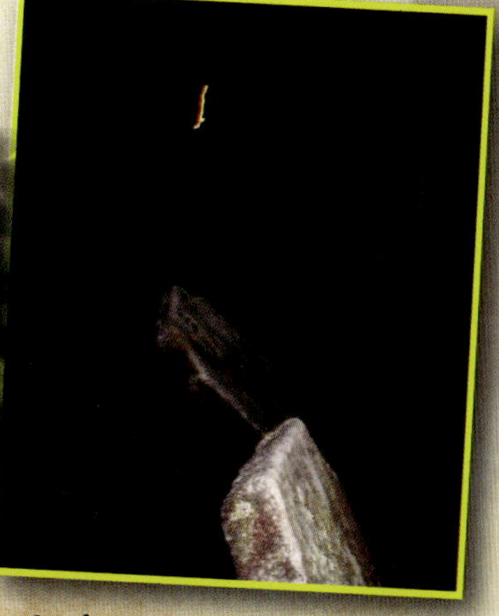

A photo taken at Union Cemetery at night

The Great Vampire Hunt

HIGHGATE CEMETERY, LONDON, ENGLAND

If a vampire is one of the undead, how could a person kill it? Folklore says sunlight will kill a vampire. So will driving a wooden stake through its heart, cutting off its head, or burning its body. No matter how you plan to kill a vampire, however, you have to find it first.

Highgate Cemetery

What better night for a vampire hunt than Friday the 13th? And what better place than Highgate, a spooky, overgrown cemetery?

In the late 1960s, many people claimed to have seen a mysterious dark figure lurking in the graveyard. Some even said they were attacked by him. Could he be a vampire, as many believed? On the evening of Friday, March 13, 1970, vampire hunters swarmed the graveyard to find out.

A vampire was not found that night, but the hunt continued for years. Tombs were broken open and wooden stakes were thrust through bodies. Corpses unearthed from the cemetery during the hunt have been discovered throughout the neighborhood. A headless body was even found sitting behind the steering wheel of a car! Some say the vampire has been driven out of Highgate. Yet the eerie sightings continue.

Since Highgate Cemetery was opened in 1839, more than 160,000 people have been buried there. Many horror movies have been filmed in the cemetery, including the classic *Taste the Blood of Dracula* (1970).

A Ghostly Keeper

LA RECOLETA CEMETERY
BUENOS AIRES, ARGENTINA

La Recoleta has wide, tree-lined streets and thousands of small, beautiful buildings and sculptures. The cemetery covers 14 acres (5.7 ha). People say it looks just like a small city—yet all the residents are dead.

There are many important and famous people buried at La Recoleta, including past presidents of Argentina.

In the early 1900s, David Allano, an Italian immigrant, was a caretaker at La Recoleta. He loved the cemetery and wanted it to be his final resting place. Throughout his life, he saved money to build an elaborate tomb. He even paid an Italian sculptor to create an image of himself in marble, with his broom, watering can, and keys. Legend says that when the tomb was finished, David took his own life. He was put to rest in his beloved cemetery. Since then, many workers have claimed to hear an unusual sound when dawn breaks in La Recoleta. It's the rattling of the ghostly caretaker's keys.

Another chilling story tells of a young man who met a pretty girl near the cemetery. He took her out for the evening. On the way home, she felt cold, so he lent her his coat. The next day, the young man went to the girl's house to collect his coat. He was alarmed to find out from the girl's mother that the girl had died years earlier and was buried at La Recoleta Cemetery. The shocked boy went to the girl's mausoleum and found his coat lying just outside her tomb. The ghost is said to be Luz María García Velloso, who died in 1925.

The tomb of Luz María García Velloso

A World of the . . .

A haunting house in Chicago, Illinois

A restless ghost in Justice, Illinois

A woman in white in Easton, Connecticut

A vampire in Exeter, Rhode Island

An angry spirit in San Diego, California

NORTH AMERICA

A ghostly battlefield in Gettysburg, Pennsylvania

A visitor to Poe's grave in Baltimore, Maryland

The Voodoo Queen in New Orleans, Louisiana

A bloody creature in Richmond, Virginia

A vampire tree in Guadalajara, Mexico

ATLANTIC OCEAN

SOUTH AMERICA

PACIFIC OCEAN

Ghost town graves in La Noria, Chile

A phantom caretaker in Buenos Aires, Argentina

SOUTHERN OCEAN

Alarming Afterlife

Glossary

afterlife the life a person has after they die

catacombs underground cemeteries made up of many tunnels and rooms

cemetery an area of land where dead bodies are buried

charms objects that people believe will bring them good luck or protect them

Civil War the United States war between the northern and southern states that lasted from 1861 until 1865

coffins containers in which dead people are placed for burying

consumption a slow wasting away of the body caused by a disease called tuberculosis

corpses dead bodies

crypt an underground room used to bury people

derelict left or deserted; abandoned

disembodied separated from or existing without a body

eerie mysterious, strange

eternal an endless time period

execution putting a person to death

folklore the traditional beliefs, stories, and customs of a group of people

funeral a ceremony that is held after a person dies

gallows a wooden structure from which people are hanged

grave a hole dug in the ground where a dead person is buried

gravestones carved stones that mark the places where people are buried

graveyards areas of land where dead bodies are buried, often connected to churches

headstones slabs of stone set up at the tops of graves

hitchhiking traveling by standing on the side of the road and asking for rides from passing vehicles, usually by sticking out one's thumb

immigrant a person who comes from one country to live in a new one

infrared a form of energy that is similar to light but can't be seen by the human eye

legend a story that is handed down from the past that may be based on fact but is not always completely true

mausoleum a burial place, usually in the form of a small building

monastery a place where people who have devoted their lives to their faith work and live

morale the mental or emotional state of a person or group

mummy the preserved body of a dead person

orbs glowing spheres

pendulum a weight that moves from side to side

phantom a ghost or spirit

pioneer a person who goes to live in a place that is not yet settled

pneumonia a disease of the lungs that makes it difficult to breathe

poltergeist a disruptive ghost that makes loud noises and moves objects

potions mixtures of liquids

quarries places in the ground or along the sides of hills from which large rocks are cut

renovated improved the condition of something

resurrection a return to life after death

saltpeter a kind of salt that occurs naturally

sea level the average height of the sea's surface

starvation to suffer or die from hunger

toast to drink in honor of someone or something

tomb a grave, room, or building in which a dead body is buried

voodoo a religion that often involves the use of charms and spells

wooden stake a piece of wood with a sharp point at one end

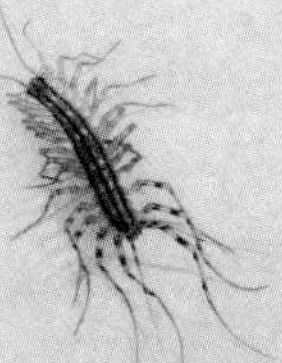

Read More

Morrison, Marie. *Gettysburg Is Haunted! (Haunted History).* New York: PowerKids Press, 2020.

Seigel, Rachel. *The Haunted History of Chicago, Illinois (Haunted History of the United States).* Minneapolis: ABDO Publishing, 2024.

Snowden, Matilda. *Investigating Ghosts in Cemeteries (Investigating Ghosts).* Hallandale, FL: Mitchell Lane Publishers, 2021.

Troupe, Thomas Kingsley. *Haunted Graveyards and Temples (The Haunted!).* New York: Crabtree Publishing Company, 2022.

Learn More Online

1. Go to **www.factsurfer.com** or scan the QR code below.
2. Enter "**Alarming Afterlife**" into the search box.
3. Click on the cover of this book to see a list of websites.

Index

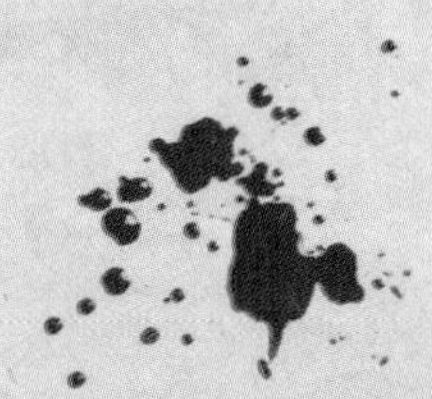

Where do you
dare NOT go?